By Kai Cheng Thom

I Hope We Choose Love:
A Trans Girl's Notes from the End of the World

a place called No Homeland

Fierce Femmes and Notorious Liars:
A Dangerous Trans Girl's Confabulous Memoir

Falling Back in Love with Being Human:
Letters to Lost Souls

FALLING
BACK IN
LOVE
WITH BEING
HUMAN

THE DIAL PRESS ··· NEW YORK

FALLING BACK IN LOVE WITH BEING HUMAN

LETTERS TO LOST SOULS

KAI CHENG THOM

Falling Back in Love with Being Human is a work of nonfiction.

A Dial Press Trade Paperback Original

Copyright © 2023 by Kai Cheng Thom

All rights reserved.

Published in the United States by The Dial Press, an imprint of
Random House, a division of Penguin Random House LLC,
New York.

THE DIAL PRESS is a registered trademark and the colophon is a
trademark of Penguin Random House LLC.

LIBRARY OF CONGRESS CATALOGING-IN-PUBLICATION DATA
Names: Thom, Kai Cheng, author.
Title: Falling back in love with being human: letters to lost souls /
Kai Cheng Thom.
Description: First edition. | New York: The Dial Press, 2023.
Identifiers: LCCN 2022035914 (print) |
LCCN 2022035915 (ebook) |
ISBN 9780593594988 (trade paperback) |
ISBN 9780593594995 (ebook)
Subjects: LCGFT: Poetry.
Classification: LCC PR9199.4.T446 L68 2023 (print) |
LCC PR9199.4.T446 (ebook) | DDC 811/.6—dc23/eng/20220818
LC record available at https://lccn.loc.gov/2022035914
LC ebook record available at https://lccn.loc.gov/2022035915

Printed in Canada on acid-free paper

randomhousebooks.com

9 8 7 6 5 4 3

Book design by Simon M. Sullivan

For all the monsters who are still waiting to be loved

Contents

FALLING
BACK IN
LOVE
WITH BEING
HUMAN

Dear Reader,

Have you ever wondered how human beings can be so contradictory—so cruel and depraved, yet so capable of kindness all at once? Have you ever struggled to hold on to these multiple truths, to your faith in the possibility of human goodness, in the face of all the chaos and conflict that we inflict upon one another?

I suspect you have, dear reader. Me too.

I've never been a stranger to ethically troubling situations. I grew up as a Chinese transgender girl in a hostile world, and my career has always brought me into contact with the harsher side of human nature. In my adolescence, I was an activist. In my twenties, I was a sex worker and then a psychotherapist. And in the past few years, I've been a conflict mediator and spiritual healer. In each incarnation of my professional life, I've pursued the same deeply personal mission: To witness the essential beauty and goodness that lives within each and every person on this planet. To live in the knowledge that everyone is both worthy of love and capable of loving. To embrace the revolutionary belief that every human being—no matter how hateful or horrible—is intrinsically sacred.

Although it's been a long time since I was a part of any organized religion, faith has always been my solace and my guide—not faith in any particular god, necessarily (though I was raised in a syncretic mix of Buddhism and Evangelical Christianity, and both the Buddha and Jesus hold tender spots in my heart), but rather faith in other people. Faith in the transformative power of the bonds between us.

Of course, my faith was tested. Isn't that always the way? The trouble with people is that unlike gods or bodhisattvas, we are only mortals, and so destined to disappoint and even harm one another.

In the past few years, I experienced some deeply personal losses and witnessed some deeply disturbing violence. In the midst of the COVID-19 pandemic and climate change and cancel culture, people seemed to be treating one another with a viciousness that threatened to shatter me. It wasn't just my world that was falling apart. It was everyone's.

So I wrote. I wrote as though I might be casting a spell or chanting a religious litany. I wrote as though *poetry* and *prayer* might mean the same thing, as if words might reconnect me with what I once considered my unshakable relationship with the human divine. I wrote to summon the language that might help me fall back in love with being human. I wrote my way through the question: *What happens when we imagine loving the people—and the parts of ourselves—that we do not believe are worthy of love?* What emerged was a series of love letters to unexpected people and places, to the parts of the world and my own self that I thought were beyond saving.

Yes, dear reader. This is a book of love letters—to dead people, to exes, to prostitutes and johns. Love letters to weirdos and monsters, to transphobes and racists, to everyone and everything I have ever had trouble holding in my heart. I needed to know that I could love them, because that meant I could still love myself—as hopeless and lost as I had become. From the depths of my rage and despair, I needed to find my way back to love.

This book is my act of prayer in a collapsing world. My devotion to the belief that we are all intrinsically sacred. My bridge back to hope.

I hope it can be yours too.

Yours in love,
Kai Cheng Thom

to the ones whose bodies shall shake the heavens

AFTER SANDY STONE

dear trans women: the only way to live as a being cast as irrevocably monstrous is to embrace a monster's power. the power to inspire awe, horror, unbidden desire. a monster is a creature made of the truth no one else dares to speak. a monster is a being beyond fear. dear trans women: when they come bearing torches, remember that you are a being born of flame. and every moment you love yourself is a moment they can never take from you. dear trans women: we are the original witches. the reincarnations of the ones they burned. lesser outcasts will turn against you to save themselves; forgive them, for they know not what they do. never forget that a lineage of monstresses stands behind you, and stands proud. dear trans women: blessed are the hideous. blessed are the horrifying. blessed are the cursed. blessed are the unforgiven, the forgotten, the ones-who-must-not-be-loved. blessed are the mad, for our bodies shall shake the heavens.

*Without looking at a dictionary,
define the word* monster.

to a lost sister

i stopped writing poems for a year after it happened. i didn't believe in them anymore because they didn't save your life. i'm not a praying woman, but poetry has always been my hotline to the universe. i guess that somewhere deep inside, i hoped that if i said something elegantly enough, it would come true. that if i spoke the language of beauty, maybe God would finally start listening. *are you there, God? it's me, fucked-up transsexual with a savior complex. i'd like you to turn back time. if i could just go back once, i'm sure i could change the past for the better.* did you know that the word *abracadabra* comes from a Hebrew phrase meaning "through speaking, i create"? i bet you do. my magic was never strong enough to manifest the miracles i wanted: to turn back time. to undo harm. to make the unspeakable things safe to say. to catch a spirit as it flies out of this world and weave it back into the body it left behind. what's the use of writing poems if they can't even do that? i wish i could talk to you. i've been wanting to tell you that complex PTSD and a crisis of faith have so much in common. they're both about losing trust in the world in the wake of unbearable loss. grief tears us away from our faith, but it's grief that brings us back as well. because in our deepest grief we have nowhere else to go. the Buddhist part of me knows that in the paradox, enlightenment is born. when you fell through a crack in the world and disappeared, i started meditating again. i lit candles every night. i tied a red rope around my waist before sleeping—anything to give my grief somewhere to go. for a year after it happened, i dreamed about getting lost in mazes and screaming without a voice, knowing that no one was coming to save me. but the Christian part of me knew that the secret of grace is choosing to believe. the secret of resilience is the art of surrender. i wish you were here. i'd tell you all the things i've learned about hope, and forgiveness, and holding on while letting go. our world keeps breaking, over and over again. i have no choice but to believe that a new one is being born.

Write a prayer of hope on a piece of paper and leave it somewhere for someone else to find.

to the ones who didn't cry

when i first heard that the gunman had walked into three
massage parlors in Atlanta and shot eight people dead, six of
whom were Asian women, i did not cry. i went to bed and
slept without dreaming, an instrument with its strings cut. it
wasn't until the morning after, as i watched the news, as i
heard the white police officer say that the shooter was "fed
up," that he'd had "a really bad day," that i felt my body break
open and the words came pouring out like a rainstorm. like
lava, like fire pouring out from deep within. tell me about the
pain of a body that knows its life means nothing. i am
learning more and more about what that means. i know i'm
not alone in the least. i want to hear the stories of gun
violence, police brutality, and racism. i want to know the
truth even as it rips me apart like a land mine. for weeks after
the shooting, whenever i tried to talk about it, i found myself
weeping instead. i think the truth was choking me as it tried
to find a way out of my throat. i want to tell you about the

white man who used to pay me for massages. i want to tell you how he said he had a sex addiction, how he became obsessed with me, how i couldn't tell anyone because they'd say it was my fault for choosing the job i did. when i saw the Asian advocacy groups talking about how it was wrong to assume that the victims of the shooting were sex workers, that it was insulting and degrading to Asian women, my body started screaming: *why is my existence degrading to you? what do i remind you of?* the news says we never got a confirmation about the kind of work those women did, and i think, *why would you tell the truth when you know what people might do with it?* Asian sisters and siblings, you can hate the plot of *Miss Saigon* without hating Miss Saigon. your body is not an invitation for violence. do you know, neither is mine. no body deserves to be silenced by bullets. no body deserves to be disposed of in the name of someone else's shame. a body is skin wrapped around stories, is tissue filled with veins that the truth runs through, is a box of bones with a voice inside. i don't want to be a volcano. i want to be a garden full of flowers bursting open toward life, all of them singing, *i'm here. i mean something. i want to live.*

Imagine a world in which all sex workers are considered sacred and holy, deserving of workers' rights, health benefits, and compensation of their choosing. Draw or paint a picture of your vision. This might be a scene or person, or more abstract: a reflection of a feeling or energy.

to the compulsive caregivers

this one's for the kids who took the role of team mom on the playground while everyone else was playing superhero and supermodel. the sweet little girls and sensitive little boys and tender little ones whose genders were still to be determined, still in flux, still contested territory. the ones who knew, with mysterious skill, exactly how to be what everyone else needed them to be. who knew in their bones how to be a mommy, a daddy, a caregiver of any gender, even though — or perhaps *because* — the big people at home who were supposed to know didn't. for the teens who were the first one that classmate with the wild hair and the dark makeup and the frightened eyes told about the things that were happening at home. the secret keepers, the unpaid crisis responders, the ones who took frantic calls at all hours of the night and went to the high school guidance counselor ostensibly for assessment for therapy, for support for the scars on their arms, but mostly to figure out how to become therapists themselves, because no adult can help a kid the way another kid can. for the ones who grew up to be social workers and nurses and psychologists and any other flavor of professional helper, because they were already doing the helping, so they might as well get paid for it too. because helping and holding and listening and caring were the only times we felt we knew what we were doing, even though we had no idea. because that was the way that other people loved us. because maybe, we thought in our secret hearts, that's all we were good for.

caregiver, i see you.

i want to tell you about all the other things you are, all the shapes that are waiting for you to come and live inside. your being is still to be determined, still in flux, still contested territory. there is knowledge in your bones about what it means to become. people are always telling that story about the statue who came to life because she loved a man. let me tell you a secret: *she came to life because she wanted to live.* it's time to be curious about what lives in the ocean of you beyond the island of other people's needs. caregiver, are you curious? what if i told you: you don't need to heal others to heal yourself, you can just heal yourself. you do not need to give love to others to love yourself, you can just love yourself. within healer and helper, there is warrior, there is priestess, there is holy whore. who knows all the things you could be?

Make a list of five good things that you frequently do for other people. Within a two-week period, do them all, at least once, for yourself.

to the girl trying to be a magic mirror when she is in fact a secret door

For the record, if you have ever done anything for attention, this poem is attention.

—ANDREA GIBSON

the first time you tried to kill yourself, you were sixteen years old. you left a letter that said, *remember you are worthy of love and capable of loving. always. always.* still trying, with a teenager's paradoxical logic, to make the world see you, even as you tried to disappear. Donald Winnicott says, *it is joy to be hidden but disaster not to be found.* nobody found you. not in the womb, when your parents were expecting a good Chinese son instead of the little fairy girl hidden inside. not in school, where the teachers saw a quiet model minority and not the raging queen you were about to become. not the straight-acting boy you fell for in the tenth grade, who called you one night to ask about homework and five minutes later burst into tears as he told you that his mother died when he was eleven and also he was secretly gay—though not for you, you were too effeminate, too freakish, too damaged for his taste. to this day, you fall for people who want to give you their woundedness but not their kindness or care. a part of you still believes that only the wounded can see the shadows you keep in the hidden compartment of your soul, and that's why you've made yourself so good at loving the wounded. when will you learn? *they come to be seen but not to see.* the alcoholic scientist with an apartment full of broken clocks. the white queers just *dying* to "learn from a trans woman of color." the sexy banker with a live-in cis girlfriend from whom he keeps you a secret. to them, you are a mirror. they look at you to discover themselves. they will never see you because that's not what they came to find. stop trying to be a mirror, silly girl. remember you are a doorway, a garden, a long twisted path that leads to an ancient temple. you are full of wildness and wilderness, of secrets passed on by the spirit of the First Femme. go hunting in your body and devour the pleasure you find there. raise your arms to the sky and swear by your sinful sacred skin, swear by your marrow, swear by the lightning storm dancing in your pelvis. swear to the boy you were and the girl you couldn't be, swear to everything you were and are and will become: *i will always find you. i will never abandon any part of you ever again.*

Design and perform a ritual to release
something from your life that you love,
but that is no longer serving you.
Throw a handful of dandelion seeds
out the window of a moving vehicle,
or clip a lock of your hair and leave it
on your windowsill for the birds to
carry away.

to the sisterhood of trans femmes

being a trans femme:

is awesome because my being and my body are pure transformative freedom.

is shitty because my freedom makes so many people afraid of me.

is amazing because i come from a lineage of change makers, magic weavers, world shakers, and warrior queens.

is painful because i never know how much of what people see when they look at me is actually me, and how much is the ghost of a monstrous transsexual they carry around in their heads.

is powerful because there isn't a cis man or woman in the world who doesn't quake before the beauty of a trans femme.

is terrifying because my power means that this world has tried to kill me again and again and again and again.

is radical because i am the roots of a vine spreading flowers throughout this world, a stretching network of sister solidarity with every fierce and fabulous femme throughout space and time.

is lonely because sometimes even your sisters don't understand you, don't see you; sometimes your sisters are the ones who cut the deepest, that's just how sisters are.

is healing because i know there is a place beyond space and time where all sisters can still forgive one another.

is hard because relationship building and relationship maintenance and relationship repair take actual labor, actual logistics, actually getting off my ass to make someone dinner or take someone to the clinic or listen to someone have a crisis on the phone.

is wonderful because i am full of wonder, because there are so many things about being a trans femme that i still long to discover, that i still need to know.

is frustrating because i still haven't figured out what it means to be a "woman," i still don't know if i am real enough, i still have yet to redefine realness in a way that makes me feel like i fully know myself; because i am still shit at nail polish and makeup and all the high femme things that i feel like i should have gotten back in 2012.

is killing me because to be a trans femme means being she-who-must-not-be-loved and all i want in this world is to be loved.

is my plan, is my purpose, is not a mistake, is a gift from the First Femme, from the goddess, from the ancestor ghosts of sisters past and sisters to come; is a mission that i will not fail, that i will always fail, sisters, this i swear, no matter how many times i fail you i will always try again and again.

being a trans femme:

is something i choose, yes, i choose this, for all its contradictions.

is choosing love.

is love.

is love.

is love.

is love.

is love.

love.

If you are a transfeminine person,
write a list of reasons you love being
a trans fem(me) and a list of
reasons you hate it.

If you are not a transfeminine person,
write a list of ways you can become
more knowledgeable about
transmisogyny and more supportive
of trans fem(me)s in your life
and the world.

to a trans femme of color child from a
trans femme of color ancestor

dearest you. know that you are not alone. never alone. even
in those moments when the world seems to open its mouth to
swallow you whole, when the daylight burns with bigotry and
the night is full of teeth, know that we are here. an army of
fierce femme ghosts stands in your wake. we are bound to
you, and you to us. bound by something greater than blood,
than bone, than flesh, than fluid. something greater than
death or disease or the hatred of a million fathers. bound
by the words of a force beyond fire, a sisterhood beyond
burning, a being-ness they could never wipe out. i call you
deathwalker, world weaver, she-who-is-summoned, storyteller,
curse bringer, blessing maker, they-who-were-chosen-by-the-
goddess. you were born to be a healer and a warrior and a
pleasure maker, to be a brightly burning azure star. you were
born to sing the end of days, the beginning of a new time. let
them come for you with their flaming branches, their hatred

and terror, their laws and their bullets and their Bibles full of a thousand lies. let them denounce you in the names of all their false gods. your divinity is not found in any book. your divinity comes from within. you have something they could never destroy. we made and remade ourselves and this world, and they fear us because we are the end of theirs. breathe a new time into being, dearest child. your will and your desire are all that you need. never surrender to the illusion that you are not enough; you are more than anyone dreamed you could be. tear down their walls and their rules and their petty false idols. write me letters in your dreams to tell me how we won. i call you dearly beloved. i call you sister and daughter and wombless mother to a thousand femmes. i call you weird and wise. when you close your eyes, when you weep, when you wonder where to run, call for me. i will be here.

Build an altar of offerings to your ancestors. What do they need in the afterlife? What are you asking for in exchange?

to all the boys i've loved before who didn't love me back

i've spent all these years thinking about how i should have known better, being angry at myself for falling for the same old bullshit cycle that Damaged Girls™ like me always seem to get stuck in: *did you ever even like me? why did you come on so strong, only to ghost at the precise moment that i let myself catch feelings? don't you know how dangerous that is? how dangerous i can be? the poetess in* White Oleander *stalked a man and poisoned him with flowers for seducing and ghosting her. that's the kind of character i've identified with since i was sixteen.* i am not a woman to be trifled with. i come from a lineage of femmes who die and rebirth ourselves, claiming the names of monstresses of legend. i'm the spiritual daughter of some seriously bad bitches. Medea killed her own children because Jason abandoned her. Medea ain't got shit on the trans girls i call sisters. and maybe that's why boys like you come to girls like me in the first place. we keep the sun in our eyes and the moon in our chests. and you? i think maybe you're a moth attracted to all that light. your words and promises crumble to dust as soon as you get too close, fall through our fingers, leaving only the taste of ash in our mouths. the first dozen times a boy used me and left me, i held on too hard. i burned the earth, i left scars behind that i'll never stop feeling guilty for. the second dozen times, i tried to collapse myself, a star turning inside out in apology for being. now i know better. i'm not sorry i loved you, i'm not sorry for wanting so much that it left scorch marks on my bones, i'm not sorry that my body still knows a desire so strong that all the racism and transmisogyny and disappointment and trauma in the world couldn't kill it. i'm not even sorry you didn't love me back. peace be to the moths, winging their way through the dark. peace be to the heavenly bodies, still tracing the same cycles a billion years after they were born. peace be to the damaged girls, the broken boys, all of us still learning what it means to hold without hurting. maybe someday you'll be ready. maybe you'll never be. either way, i'll be in the woods after midnight, searching for fireflies without a mason jar, hoping to catch one by standing still and holding out my open hands.

Write a letter to someone you
loved who didn't love you back.
Go somewhere beautiful and burn
the letter. Treat yourself to
something nice.

to the confabulists

Lying is the work of those who have been taught
that their truths have no value.

—AMBER DAWN

i was seven years old when i told my first lie, and i still
remember how it tasted: salty, savory, delicious, dirty, divine,
dangerous, powerful, like freedom. how it came from
nowhere, from the empty air, from a secret place inside my
body that i'd never even known was there. how it felt electric,
alive, like turning a key in a lock and stepping into the light.
here was magic. here was escape. here was the power to twist
reality with nothing but words, *abracadabra alakazam,*
through the act of speaking, i create. here was shapeshifting,
becoming someone else. with a lie you become lovable, at
least for a while, until you're discovered and everything turns
to dust once again. this is the miracle. this is how pathological
liars come to be. the gift of the Lightbringer, legacy of the

Morning Star: *mythomania. pseudologia fantastica.* the secret art through which storytellers and confabulists are born. lie because you have to. lie to survive. lie because it feels good, because it's so much more bearable than inhabiting the truth, because the truth will get you killed if you're a faggot fairy child with hollow bird bones. oh, liars, oh, longing ones, visioners of alternative truths. it takes one to know one. perhaps this is why i've always been drawn to religion, to cults, to narcissist leaders of revolutionary movements, even after i devoted my life to honesty. i know what it means to get high on your own supply. the incredibly addictive rush of blind faith. inside every lie there is a deeper truth, a germ of the reality the speaker wishes could be. dear confabulist, do you know the difference between propaganda and poetry? one is a lie that takes you further away from the truth, and the other is a lie that takes you closer to it. politics, art, spirituality, healing: all a maze of mirrors and fog that will devour you if you let it. allow me to give you an ex–compulsive liar's wisdom: find the lie in your heart. the one you tell to yourself and all the world, sometimes without even knowing it. pare that lie down to its barest core, strip back the skin, and behold the truth: *i am worthy of love and capable of loving. i am capable of loving and worthy of love.* you never lied, and neither did i—not really, not in our hearts. i believe you, dear one, i believe you. no need to say a word. i believe you. i believe you. i believe i believe i believe.

Think of a lie you've told about yourself. Summon the memories of all the times this lie felt true. What does this lie reveal about who you really are?

to the fantasy man i still long for

healer, i need you, i've been waiting all night. healer, i'm
calling you with all my might. healer wanted: a man who can
talk about not only his feelings but also mine. someone who
asks questions. someone curious. someone whose body craves
the ocean and whose hands know a soft touch. split me open
with those hands, healer, pluck me like a flower that blossoms
once a year beneath the hungry summer stars. hold me with
hands that know how to speak in the sacred language of scars.

healer, i need you, i've been waiting all night. healer, i'll
wait till the morning light. healer wanted: someone sweet
and soft who believes in what's right. tell me you're out
there, healer. you're not just fantasy. as i dream of you,
you're somewhere dreaming of me. healer, have you
waited as i have? have you wanted and wished for a woman
who is wicked, a woman who is wild, a woman who gets
what she wants? are you ready, healer, have you paved the

way? have you lit the candles and chanted the words? have you cast a ring of flower petals around your bed? have you heard the call of the screech owl, do you know her secret face? have you summoned me to knock down your doors and tear off your clothes and enter your body like a golden moonbeam piercing the sapphire flesh of the sky?

healer, i need you, i've been waiting all night. i need a healer who knows a thousand names for Delight. healer wanted: one who needs me. do you need me, healer? do you know it? speak the words of the boundless wanting that swells like salt waves inside you. look in the mirror and call me by your name. tell the truth of who you are and what you want, and wait for me to appear.

Think of a person in your life who actively cares for you. Find a way to show your gratitude.

to the deathwalkers

*It's not desiring the fall; it's terror of the flames. And yet
nobody down on the sidewalk, looking up and yelling 'Don't!'
and 'Hang on!', can understand the jump. Not really. You'd
have to have personally been trapped and felt flames to really
understand a terror way beyond falling.*

—DAVID FOSTER WALLACE, *Infinite Jest*

this poem is not here to try to force you to live. there are no
words on this earth that could force you to live, not if you
really wanted to go. that's something this poem learned the
hard way, trying its best to play the part of the wise healer, all-
knowing Earth Mother, sitting with dozens of queer children,
dancing on the filament between life and death. it always
comes down to *i can't let you leave*. to calling the cops if it
comes to that. this poem remembers the cops. the handcuffs
they put around its adolescent wrists that day, supposedly to
save its life. this poem remembers the locked room, the

psychiatrist with his metal desk and no-nonsense metal questions. this poem remembers the steely waiver the principal made it sign promising that if it attempted again, it would not be on school property, for liability reasons, of course. so many stratagems to force this poem to live, so few to make life feel worthwhile. this poem is not here to force you to live. this poem is not made of metal. this poem is made of soft grass and dried flowers, sweet-smelling herbs and petrified wood. this poem is a magic circle that is strong enough to hold the weight of your truth, that this world is unbearable and sometimes you can't bear it. this poem is an acknowledgment of the deep wisdom of all your most shameful and exiled parts. this poem is a promise to never stop believing in the inherent worthiness of everything you were and are and could choose to be. this poem knows you are afraid. this poem is afraid too. once, for a whole year, this poem wore a silver pendant with poison pills inside, just to know that it had the option to leave. deathwalker, this poem is here to honor you. it sees you and your suffering. there is nothing in this world that could make this poem stop wanting you to stay. this poem is here to tell you, *you matter. you*

would be missed. you are worth fighting for. you are worthy.
you are important. you are precious. you are so, so brave. this
world is a burning building. whether you leap from a high
window or face the flames, know that i am here with you.
burning.

Gather some small pieces of paper. On each piece, write down one thing that you like about the world. Fill a jar with dried flower petals and your pieces of paper. When you are feeling down, pull one of the pieces of paper out of the jar to remind yourself of what you love about living.

to the church of social justice

Then said Jesus unto him, Put up again thy sword into his place: for all they that take the sword shall perish with the sword.

—Matthew 26:52 (King James Version)

i was three years old the first time someone told me i was going to hell. i was born into a Chinese Evangelical community on my mother's side, and the figures of God and the devil loomed large. they didn't seem so different to me then: the devil, with his deceit and temptations, and God, with his commandments and judgments and conditional love. i mean, they say he'll always forgive you, but they also say he has a lake of fire and if you sin and don't repent you'll burn in it for all of time, which is kind of a mixed message if you ask me. so i left Christianity and found radical art and politics. found queer community. found the good word of social justice. i was seventeen years old the first time a group of radical activists sat me down in a basement in Montreal and told me my questions were problematic. they said i had to believe, and i had to act on those beliefs in all the right ways, or else i had chosen the side of the oppressor. i've always been a good believer. i've always been good at speaking the word, because you see, i know about words. their mystery, their power. their shadow side, their wickedness. i was born with a forked tongue, a limp wrist, a mysterious dark mark on my skin. i know deceit and temptation. i know commandment and judgment. i know the flaming sword and the angel. i know conditional love and what it takes to keep it. the radical queers said there was room for everybody in the movement, that no one was disposable. they also said that if someone was problematic and didn't repent, they could be publicly shamed and punished indefinitely, which is kind of a mixed message if you ask me. still, i look for God. still, i look for goodness, forgiveness; i look for guidance in the word. my faith didn't last, but it granted me grace. my politics betrayed me, but they still provided purpose. what am i now in this world without them?

not a social justice warrior, but a social justice wonderer. a
social justice wanderer. somebody, anybody, grant this girl
sanctuary. i have questions about heaven. i have questions
about the Revolution. those questions are the same: *upon
whose bones do you intend to build your paradise?*

Take yourself somewhere quiet and comfortable and reflect on one personality trait within yourself that bothers you. What bothers you about it? How do you feel when you notice this quality in others? How would you feel if this personality trait within you was smaller, quieter, or gone altogether?

to Jesus Christ

i've been rekindling an affair with my old boyfriend Jesus Christ. we've grown apart and back together and apart again over the years, but it's sweet and it's familiar, and right now, it's exactly what i need. he's not the sharpest knife in the drawer, that Jesus. he could have made smarter investments than *the spiritual redemption of all humankind.* but he's an idealist, which i like. he's a deep thinker and just a tiny bit self-involved. he's got daddy issues, which, to be honest, i also like. he's got a nice face and a hairy chest and moves with gangly, long-limbed grace. he's a bit of a yoga bro, a brocialist too. always quoting Karl Marx like socialism was invented yesterday. he's a softboi, my Jesus, a fixer-upper for sure, but he's got good bones. he likes to smoke weed and mansplain to me: how sex workers are actually a lot like therapists without the job security or the respect. how capitalism is an unsustainable socioeconomic framework that can only lead to societal collapse over time. how the prison industrial complex is a racist construct that doesn't really bring about safety or justice. sometimes i roll my eyes at him and say, *tell me something i don't know.* sometimes i just jump on those good bones, tackle him to the ground, and we roll around laughing. the sex is good. Jesus likes getting pegged. he looks younger in the midst of pleasure, and sometimes after sex he cries, and i don't know if he's just happy to reconnect or sad because we both know that things will never work out between us long-term. i really wanted them to. i wanted to curl up in those long arms and long legs, to recline into Jesus's sweet, fuzzy chest and bask in that dopey, gentle affection for all of linear time. i wanted to be saved, but i'm not that kind of girl. there's something sharp inside me that even the Son of God can't smooth out. and it hurts, because i once wanted so much to be the kind of girl who was worthy of salvation, who could just let herself be saved. sometimes i'm the one who cries afterward. and he just holds me, my Jesus, and strokes

my hair with his carpenter's hands that still bear scars
where they nailed him to the cross. and i say, *tell me
something i don't know.* and he says, *grace is the divine love
that all beings are worthy to receive, even in light of all we've
done wrong.*

Write a letter of forgiveness to someone. That someone can be yourself.

to the runaways

we were just children when we left to find the pack. hunted
and haunted, already half feral, we knew even then we were
better suited to life among canids than *Homo sapiens*, with
their labyrinth of cages and hard light. we took to the
shadows, stood waiting in the wet grass, bathed in the greedy
glow of the razor moon. we slunk through the alleyways,
climbed fences, and scaled rooftops. we darted across
highways in the dead of the night. risked death in the
headlights of heterosexuals who couldn't be bothered to stop
for a wayward faggot, tranny, or dyke. followed the scent of
burning lavender and cigarettes and desire. sooner or later,
we sniffed one another out. we picked one another up in
abandoned buildings and empty fields, twining body around
body, marking our territory by tooth and by nail. oh, how we
hunted. and oh, how we ran. we ran like the river running
through the old industrial part of town, full of poison and
memory and mysterious treasure. we ran like time running

from the hands of the clock. we ran like blood running through the veins of history into the roots of the trees that rise from this land. we ran like tears running down the cheeks of the goddess of mercy. we ran like tongues running up the insides of thighs to unravel the wet center of a body in pleasure. we hunted and we haunted, and oh, how we wanted. hunger howled in our bellies like a wild living thing. by hunger we were bound, and by hunger, unwound. who can say where the slaughter began? one after another, we turned on one another. gorged ourselves on the guts of the guilty, the filthy, the shameful sinful among us. which is to say, every one of us. we had blood on our teeth; we bore the mark of the beast. we skinned our leaders and lovers and hung the meat from the trees. this is how a body in trauma tears itself apart. we eat ourselves. we devour our siblings and bury the remains where they'll never be found. somewhere out there, our ghosts are still running.

Go somewhere you have
never been before.

to the martyrs

You do not have to be good.

— MARY OLIVER, "Wild Geese"

you come from a long line of round-the-clock workers: single moms slinging burgers during the day and operating the phone sex line at night, taxi drivers doing sixteen-hour shifts, the immigrant owners of twenty-four-hour corner stores with no employees who aren't members of the family. there are a thousand variations on this theme, but the outcome on your spirit is the same. you found your way to community organizing, to church volunteer work, to political advocacy, with the fiery devotion of a zealot. there's nothing you wouldn't do, nothing you wouldn't give, not a sacrifice in the world you wouldn't make for your cause. you took the hands-on, unglamorous work of change-making and raised it to the level of religion. your labor was herculean. like the horse, you said, *i will work harder.* stood atop the slow-burning pyre of the Revolution and set yourself ablaze. *i will burn harder.* you never thought to ask if the Revolution needed more than your ashes to be made real. dear martyr, do not wonder what you would be outside of your great labors. you already know exactly what you are: body lying by the ocean, listening to the sound of the waves. body dancing to the sound of a guitar on the street in front of a café at two o'clock in the morning. body nestled against the warm bare chest of a person who makes you laugh and cry and come. body resting. body reading. body being, more than doing. body weeping. body dreaming. body knowing exactly what it wants and needs in every moment of every day. body like a sacred animal, body close to the divine. dear martyr, somewhere deep inside you've always believed that you were called to do the work of a higher purpose. but you do not need to walk a hundred miles on your knees. you need only to fall on them. you do not need to burn in repentance for all the things you couldn't be, couldn't do; all the ones you couldn't save. you need only to let yourself be saved. you do not need to build a grand and glorious temple to love. your body is the temple to love.

*Adorn your body with
something beautiful.*

to the goddess of whores and all her children

i can offer only my own story, Goddess. my own body, one
small gem in this ancient chain. this net of jewels cast among
all those who have walked the petaled path, plying our trade
in the shadow of the rose. i kneel before my altar and fan a
stack of cash, light the candles and say the words. i press my
hands together, and whore magic pours from the cracks in
my palms.

yes, i romanticize it. i glamorize the work. it's what i knew i
had to do to survive it and thrive in it. playing at priestess
in the tiny battered temple of my studio apartment.
adorned in the finest raiments Victoria's Secret could offer.
anointed in drugstore makeup. i named myself after you,
Goddess, and summoned good fortune. hear this: good
fortune came. it came with the first man, and the man
after that. and with the man after that and the man after

that. like manna it came, as though falling from the sky to
answer my prayers. how could i fail to become one of yours
in the wake of such a miracle?

the gift you gave us was the power of touch. how
many people have passed through my hands? my body
kept the score. i still have the taste of them, the smell, the
feel of their skin. i keep the memory of each one inside
me. like foxes, like wolves, like coyotes they came,
canine in their hunger and heat. i tamed them, Goddess.
i used the gifts you gave me. i opened them up. skinned
them alive. wove them back together and returned them
from the dead. made them human again. made them
whole. you taught me that, Goddess: what pleasure
can do.

there are so many more stories, whore stories, to tell. but
tonight i want magic, glamour, gloss. i want to pay homage
to streetside angels and motel priestesses, the webcam
Glorianas and trick-turning witches. i want to give honor to

us, guardians of sacred intimacy. i want to bear witness to those we lost along the way. i want to sing hosanna to us, the ones who survived. i offer this to the goddess, my body's prayer: *whores, you are holy. never forget. holiness, thy name is whore.*

Give yourself one full night of self-pleasure. Define self-pleasure however you like.

to the johns

this is for the Jasons, the Daves, the Matthews, the Johns. the Peters, the Pauls, the Andrews, the Toms. why so many of you insist on pseudonyming yourselves after apostles is a delicious mystery i'll never fully understand. you're no saints, that's for sure. not when you haggled and scoffed and turned up your noses at an honest whore's rates, not when you made three-hour appointments and then never showed up. not when you demanded more bang for your buck, left shitty reviews deriding a woman's body on the hobbyist forums—no, you certainly weren't holy men then. not when you robbed us. not when you raped us. not when you got "just a little" too attached and stalked us for days, sent us pleading emails from a hundred fake addresses. no, sir, there was certainly nothing sanctified about that.

and yet.

most of you are courteous, and many of you are kind. so many of you are gentle, and generous, and full of the desire to give. full of longing to receive as well, and terrified at the prospect. all of you, beneath the surface, terrified and tender, and in that frightened tenderness, yes, full of grace. dear John, dear Jason, dear Matthew, dear Paul. i thought i knew about men before i became a whore. i knew stalking, i knew violence, i knew abandonment, i knew rape. i thought i might as well get paid for it. here's what i didn't know: that i could get paid to be treated like my attention was important. that an hour of my time was worth three hundred dollars or more. that my beauty, my body, my intelligence, my humor, my hands, could open one of you up and make you human again.

dear Jason, you were a twenty-eight-year-old banker who just wanted to spend some time with a woman who loved your soft cock. dear Bartholomew, you were a forty-five-year-old writer struggling with loneliness and alcoholism, and you spent most of our time talking, with clothes on. dear Peter, you were a seventy-two-year-old retiree on a fixed income who still, somehow, found six hundred dollars to spend on me in one weekend, and the first thing you wanted to do was slow dance. dear Thomas, you were a sixty-seven-year-old former farmer struggling with his young son's addiction issues, and you brought me cherry tomatoes from your garden. dear Simon, you were an aspiring journalist who brought me a different gift every time; i still keep the black candle on a table by my bed. dear Philip, you ran away the first time i opened the door, only to come back sheepishly an hour later. dear Matthew, i'm sorry i couldn't replace your wife. dear Andrew, you gave me a one-thousand-dollar tip so i'd spend the night with you one week before your wedding; i hope that, somehow, you are happy. dear James, you were my first-ever clergyman, and i am so, so honored that you chose me to sin with.

dear johns, this is for the sweet spirit we found together. the part of you i saw as age and trauma and weariness melted beneath the heat of our touch, revealing the transcendent gasping singing moaning sobbing glorious naked beauty of you. why does a man come to see a whore? he comes to find the light inside himself, and i saw that light, i still see it in you. remember your light, dear johns. keep your light alive. the world needs more of it.

Think of your ideal intimate experience. What would it be like to see someone who could give that to you with skill and kindness and without judgment? What would you be willing to exchange for that experience? Speak your answer aloud, even if only to an empty room.

to the trans exclusionary radical feminists

*I contend that the problem of transsexualism would best be
served by morally mandating it out of existence.*

—JANICE RAYMOND, *The Transsexual Empire*

this i promise you: i do not now, nor have i ever, wanted you
to stop existing. i do not want to invade or destroy that which
is sacred to you. i do not want to steal your children. i do not
want to steal your body; i have a body of my own. i do not
want you to die. i also do not want to die. dear radical
feminist, hand on my heart, this i swear: i am not the end of
your world. the world i dream of is big enough for both of us.
it is a world where neither of us needs to die at the hands of a
lover in the middle of the night with no one to answer our
screams for help. it is a world where neither of us needs to
scratch and scrabble for a place in a shelter grudgingly paid
for by a government that does not care about us. it is a world

where neither of us needs to fear rape in a prison, because no woman is deemed disposable enough to be put in a prison.

                    radical feminist, dear one, i know so much more about sisterhood than you might think. i grew up with a sister, we were born eighteen months apart. and because our parents' pride was spread so thin, we fought each other for it, and then we fought *for* each other, and then we fought each other again. over and over till the bond between us became so frayed it broke completely. still, i remember clinging to my sister in the closet as our mother raged and threatened. i remember her hand in mine as she led me around the playground, protecting me from the boys. i remember standing between her and my father's hands, protecting her from him. i remember how she would break my toys afterward, because she hated what needing to be protected felt like. you see, radical feminist, i know what it means to have a sister and be a sister. it means a bond so frayed and so thin, so twisted up in knots, that you forget how much you need it to keep you from falling, only for it to catch you once again when you least expect. it means a bond broken like a promise beneath your father's rage and your mother's hands. it means sometimes you don't speak for ten long years, but the memory of what you once meant to each other lingers on and on. dear trans exclusionary radical feminist, i know the meaning of broken trust, don't you? i know that we are more likely to survive in a world we make together, don't you? i am willing to put my fear aside in the name of a better future for girls like you and girls like me, are you, are you? i am willing to take the first step into the space between us. are you? hand on my heart, sister, this i swear: despite all that has happened, i believe we can be sisters still.

Start a conversation that you have been putting off with someone important to you.

to J. K. Rowling

If you could come inside my head and understand what I feel when I read about a trans woman dying at the hands of a violent man, you'd find solidarity and kinship. I have a visceral sense of the terror in which those trans women will have spent their last seconds on earth.

—J. K. ROWLING

When you throw open the doors of bathrooms and changing rooms to any man who believes or feels he's a woman . . . then you open the door to any and all men who wish to come inside.

—J. K. ROWLING

i wish you wouldn't fear me. if you could come inside my head and understand what i feel when i read the words of a cis woman who's terrified that the coming of my liberation means the ending of hers, then you'd find your mirror image, trying to break out of the frame. it does not do to dwell on nightmares and forget to live and let live, dear Joanne. i don't want to exist in a world where i am afraid of you, where you are afraid of me, where i am afraid of what men will do when you are afraid of me. believe it or not, i know something about being a woman. i know what it's like to live in a body defined by what men can take from it. i lived in terror too, like you. i know what being a survivor is, i know what being a survivor does, i know about the things we become in the dark, what fear turns us into when we are desperate to live. *vol de mort* means "flight from death," doesn't it, Joanne? your wicked wizard broke his soul into seven separate pieces, drank the blood of the innocent and snake's milk, and started wars, all in the name of escaping death. fear makes monsters of us all. you wrote so many monsters, so many magical creatures, and yet you still don't seem to know what a monster is, Joanne. a monster is a part of ourselves that we don't want to find in the mirror. a part of ourselves we try to cut out and split off and put inside other people so that they can carry it for us: our fear. our shame. these are Dark Arts of the oldest kind. dear Joanne, what spells are stronger than the Dark Arts? what magic did it take to end hatred, stop a war, break an Unforgivable Curse? not an easy riddle, but i bet between the two of us, we could figure it out. you and me, survivors both. you and me, students of enchantment. you and me, and the army of girls and women between us, all of us monsters and witches, the Ones Who Lived.

Read a children's book you used to love. Do you still love it?

to the ones who hurt me

i forgive you   i forgive you   i forgive you

  i forgive you   i forgive you   i forgive you

    i forgive you   i forgive you   i forgive you

i forgive you

  i forgive you

    i forgive you   i forgive you   i forgive you

i forgive you   i forgive you   i forgive you

              i forgive you

  i forgive you   i forgive you   i forgive you

i forgive you   i forgive you   i forgive you

i forgive you   i forgive you   i forgive you

          i forgive you

i forgive you   i forgive you   i forgive you

          i forgive you   i forgive you   i forgive you

          i forgive you

i forgive you   i forgive you   i forgive you

          i forgive you   i forgive you   i forgive you

i forgive you   i forgive you

i forgive you   i forgive you   i forgive you

          i forgive you   i forgive you   i forgive you

i forgive you   i forgive you   i forgive you

i forgive you   i forgive you

i forgive you   i forgive you   i forgive you

i forgive you   i forgive you   i forgive you

Collect a bag of stones. Give each stone the name of something you've been holding on to that you'd like to let go of. Take the stones to a river or ocean and drop them in.

to the ones who watched

Justice is what love looks like in public.

—CORNEL WEST

you were the only ones i couldn't forgive. it's strange, it took me almost no time at all to let go of my rage toward the men who sexually assaulted me. it happened so many times, and i rarely thought of revenge. once, i was physically attacked in public, strangled from behind by a stranger, and it never once occurred to me to be angry. the way i grew up, violence was like the weather: a lightning strike, a monsoon, ferocious and tragic, yes, but also something to be expected. you prepared for it, you endured it. you picked up the pieces and moved on. so that's what i did. and the fury that stayed with me wasn't about the assailants, the abusers, the perpetrators. it was about everyone around me who watched and did nothing.

well, not quite nothing. you gossiped about it. whispered about it. told lurid tales about it. picked sides and made innuendos and cooked up pious opinions, waving your banners of judgment: *innocent! guilty! wicked! righteous!* over and over, an endless cacophony. you made what happened to me worse, because you turned it into melodrama, a soap opera for your entertainment and education. i want you to know: my body is not your entertainment. my life is not your education.

do you want to know the truth? you were the ones i wished vengeance upon. i wanted to look into the eyes of the people who hurt me and see into their souls, i wanted to braid flowers into their hair and bathe them in healing herbs. but the bystanders? i wanted to ride on a dragon and set fire to your homes. i wanted to plant my teeth in the earth so that hydras would spring up to come after you. i wanted you to feel how i felt: consumed by an insatiable, burning demon to whom my personhood never mattered.

you, the clamoring, hungering mob, multiheaded and
faceless, you were the beast that stalked my nightmares,
and every time another celebrity is convicted in the court
of #MeToo and the crowd goes wild, i want to scream:

where were you and your righteousness when those girls were
being raped and killed? where were your demands for social
change and justice before the attack, while the violence was
happening? where were all my activist friends when i was
being groomed and used and lied to and tortured? where
were you then?

only to remember all the times i also did nothing. the
time when i was nineteen and one of my best friends
told me he'd thrown his boyfriend down the stairs and
i did nothing. the time when another friend punched his
partner in the ribs at a party and we did nothing. the time
a trans woman was sexually assaulted and murdered
in public and the whole city of queer activists did
nothing.

and then i remember why i still reach for you, the ones who watched as i was hurt. why i'm still trying to believe, to hope against hope. why despite all the rage in my heart i'm still trying to make peace with "communities" that allow violence to happen. because despite all my denials, in the end, i'm still nothing more and nothing less than one of you.

Share a meal with a small group of people you're close with. Tell each person why they're important to you.

to the goddess of vengeance and the goddess of mercy

Prison abolition is more than a politic, it's a daily practice.

—SHIRA HASSAN

my boyfriend tells me he has a friend who beats up abusers
on behalf of the people they've harmed. my boyfriend's voice
swells with admiration as he tells me this; i think he too wants
to be an avenging angel whose wings fill the night with the
sound of a justice that the courts and cops will never bring us.
i understand. i've fallen before the goddess of vengeance too.
i've felt her flaming sword and chain of skulls in my hands.
there's so much strength in rage and in the things rage wants
us to do. sometimes rage feeds you when nothing else will,
keeps you alive when everything and everyone else would
have let you die. it's possible to live on a diet of rage and
nothing else for years. it leaves you starving with a mouth full
of flame. it's not that i don't believe in punishment—quite

the opposite, in fact. i know that revenge is powerful beyond measure. it can make people hear you, see you, listen at last. it can make supremacists and conquerors tremble. this is why i fear the goddess of vengeance. she is beautiful and terrible. she demands your whole being in exchange for her gifts. i want to ask this vigilante my boyfriend admires so much: who decides? who decides when the punishment is over, when justice has been served? who decides who is worthy of the power to punish, to take life in their hands? i want to ask this same question of the cops. the courts. the people who made prisons. i want to ask where the right to violence comes from, who grants it, who makes the distinction between *violence for justice* and *violence for domination*. i understand why so many revolutionaries have chosen the goddess of vengeance. there are only three things she cannot do: turn bad people into good ones, turn harm doers into healers, turn violence into safety. every night i fall on my knees before the goddess of mercy: *this i pray. may the harm i suffered be healed. may the harm i have done be healed. may it be so. may it be so. may it be so.*

*Think of someone you'd like to punish.
If it's safe to do so, send them a book of
poetry instead. If not, read the book
yourself and share it with a friend.*

to the exiled

sometimes i think of you as a warrior of old falling upon your sword in an act of tragic honor. sometimes i imagine you as a priestess of the old religion, walking into the woods to lie beneath the trees and wait for the animals and the winds to carry away your sins, your shame. once, i had a dream that you were a sea captain who set fire to the sails of your ship. i want to know that you deserved what you got, except there's no way to know that for sure. why do all my fantasies about redemption end in sacrifice and death? is it the influence of Christ the Savior, his words still whispering in my supposedly anarchist ears, still guiding me toward the reenactment of a single story? is it something inherent to the nature of trauma and violence, an instinctive embodied belief that only the suffering of a sinner can take the suffering of the innocent away? in all my witchy wanderings, i have never known such a miracle to come true, and yet something deep inside me still yearns for the ancient rituals of cleansing and repentance. such a simple equation: the price for giving pain is to receive pain. the remedy for dishonorable deeds is death, whether symbolic or real. if only it were so easy. i wonder what it would be like to live in a different mythology. i want to think of you as a soldier, fallen from grace, who throws your sword and your armor into a sacred river, then dives in yourself and arises reborn, sworn never to draw blood again. i want to think of you as a fallen priestess who builds a cottage by the sea and spends your days in silence, growing medicinal herbs in your garden. i want to dream of a world where instead of building prisons, we build healing temples. i want to sing the stories that tell not of the cleansing power of blood, but the transformative power of tears. somewhere out in the vast universe, there must be a place where the exiled gather in humility and honesty to tend to the wounds in our souls and the wounds in the world. a place beyond punishment or even redemption. a place where all things can be seen and held for what they are. and in this life or the next, someday i'll meet you there.

Go into the woods or a nearby park and let yourself take to the earth like a fallen tree. Cover yourself in flowers, grass, or leaves. Lie on the ground and feel anything you need to feel. When you are ready, rise from the dead and go home. Have a cup of tea.

to the ones who disappeared

I believe we can be witnessed to death.

—NINA ARSENAULT

i still feel you in me all the time. at night in the space
between dreaming and wakefulness, in the space between
inhalation and exhalation. sometimes i want so much to be
with you that i forget to breathe in my sleep. my boyfriend
and partner tell me they're worried i have sleep apnea, but i
think that's just a fancy way of saying i can't let go of my
ghosts. of you, the ones who disappeared. found dead on a
street corner in the "bad" part of town. found dead in a
ravine in a park. found dead in your apartment, killed by a
client. found dead in a bathtub with your eyes gouged out.
left town and never heard from again. developed psychosis
and vanished, never to resurface again. never found. never
found. never found. a few years ago, i learned the art of
controlled hyperventilation, breathing through the mouth so

fast that the carbon dioxide level in the blood drops to below normal levels, reducing the absorption of oxygen in the brain and resulting in altered states of consciousness. as i convulsed and shuddered in that place between living and dying, i heard you singing in the void, felt you screaming through my body in wordless grief, in soundless rage. i heard you, sisters, saying over and over, *we wanted to live. we wanted to live. we wanted to live.* kindred, i wanted you to live. i don't want to live in a time where i survived and you didn't. i don't want to live knowing that my mothers and sisters were hunted and haunted, witnessed to death by a forest of eyes that looked at us and saw something so beautiful it made them want to destroy us. sometimes i don't want to live at all. i still haven't forgiven myself for surviving. maybe i never will. i inhale and i take in life. i exhale and i surrender. come, kindred, breathe through me. see through my eyes and speak through my lips. love through these hands that still know your names. trace your memory on the skin of the world. in my living body, there is life for you too, and when my last breath leaves, we will be together again.

Take one hundred gentle breaths.
With every inhalation, think: I am
alive. *With every exhalation, think:*
And I know it.

to a girl who has forgotten who she is in the fog of late-stage digital capitalism

tonight you choose yourself, silly girl. so what if you weren't your first choice? maybe you tried calling your life partner, your three handsome boyfriends, a Grindr hookup, and a few best friends, but as it turns out, they all had plans, and now you have no one to save you from the despondent languishing hell that is being alone with your thoughts. so choose yourself. read alone in a lamplit room, the way you once spent hours as a child, only to find that now it's impossible to disappear into the plot of a novel the way you once did, and eventually realize that you're tearing the pages out and crushing them in your fists, setting some on fire and throwing others out the window to flutter down to the street like lovelorn birds. breathe, silly girl. sit down on the meditation cushion you paid too much money to order from an eco-friendly online alternative health store, and close your eyes.

notice your body.

notice the sensations, emotions, and thoughts.

notice yourself noticing.

notice that you are now stabbing the meditation cushion with your sharpest kitchen knife till the bougie buckwheat filling pours out through the tears like blood. silly girl. how did you get here? still living amid the hungry ghosts of a collapsing empire. what would your ancestors, starving in rural China, say about you now? is this what they dreamed about when they came to the Golden Mountain? you, silly girl, with a shabby apartment full of books you never read, a job you can't explain in under five minutes, a bathtub full of flower petals, and a set of radical politics that seems further from reality every day? your father was right about you. silly girl. foolish girl.

useless girl.

empty-headed girl.

daydreaming girl.

nightwalking girl.

girl who was never meant to exist but breathed herself into being on the strength of her desire alone. girl who was never meant to be touched or wanted but once made her living on nothing but beauty and the magic in her hands. girl who is still haunted. girl who is still here. girl who was made for this life, made to live, no matter what her father said. girl who refused to disappear. tonight you choose yourself, silly girl. you were always worth more than you let yourself believe.

Spend twenty-four hours alone.

to the Animorphs

*Always people die in wars. And always people are left
shattered by the loss of loved ones.*

—K. A. APPLEGATE, letter to Animorphs fans

you couldn't tell us who you were or where you lived. it was
too risky. you had to be careful, really careful. so did i. so did
we, all of us queer kids growing up in the shadow of the AIDS
crisis. like you, we were children at war with an enemy that
invaded our loved ones from within. like you, we kept secrets
to protect ourselves, never knowing what might happen if the
truth should fall into the hands of enemies who might be
anyone—anywhere—anytime. a child who keeps secrets to
survive becomes a soldier in their soul. we acquired new
shapes to disguise our true forms, shifted flesh and molded
bone to afford ourselves power and protection: some of us
chose the dull camouflage of forest insects, others the fangs
and claws of beasts too terrifying to get close to. some of us

grew wings that could carry us up and away, riding the thermals to escape the pain of our bodies down below. but of course there was danger in that. what happens when you spend too long in a morph? well, you get stuck there, as Tobias discovered all those years ago. you get trapped in one shape and run the risk of forgetting what you used to be. every queer child chooses their own way to fight the war to survive. like Jake, some of us became leaders. like Rachel, some of us became fighters. like Marco, strategists. like Cassie, pacifists. like Ax, orphans. and like you, we won our war, or so they tell us now. hooray for gay marriage! faggots and trannies can get jobs and have babies and pay taxes just like everybody else. but who did we leave behind? what did we lose on the way here? one war just leads right to the next. dear Animorphs, i loved you because you never pretended that winning a battle doesn't come with a price. and still you believed in the beauty and mystery hidden deep within the bodies of all that changes and all that lives. i too still believe. that transformation is possible. that what we do here matters. that in the midst of all this monstrosity and sacrifice and terror and loss, there is still something worth fighting for.

*Learn some facts about one animal
that inspires you. Spend a few minutes
pretending to be that animal.*

to the sidekicks

all we really wanted was to be a superhero's teen sidekick.
Robin was the first to jump into the fray. he started fighting
crime at Batman's side at the tender age of eight, seeking to
avenge the death of his parents. bizarrely, he battled in wing
tip shoes and hot pants while living as Dick Grayson,
the teenage ward of billionaire Bruce Wayne, fueling infinite
Freudian nightmares across North America for decades to
come. Kid Flash, Wonder Girl, Aqualad, Superboy, Batgirl,
and four more Robins followed in Dick's footsteps.
psychologists debated whether this was menacing
homosexual subtext, but to us nerdy queer kids it was sacred
text, and it was all that we yearned for. what lonely misfit
child doesn't long to be uplifted by a powerful outsider,
granted the gift of power and mentorship, protection and
adventure, a parent and a friend, all at the same time? but
most of us were not chosen. our superhero mentors never

arrived to rescue us, train us, fight by our sides. yet still we were called to do our part on the front lines in the battle for justice. we did peer support, suicide intervention, and harm reduction for other teens; we held schoolyard GSA rallies and campaigns that were attended by a handful of outcasts and a semi-closeted teacher. at night we waited by our bedroom windows, on apartment rooftops, in abandoned playgrounds, sending psychic signals into the sky. waiting for them to find us. no one came. we were a generation of sidekicks with no heroes to guide us—where did they go? so many were killed, murdered, lost to the virus. others were disillusioned, brokenhearted, burned out of the fight. some sold out and went corporate. others fought on, but our numbers were legion, and theirs were too few to get to us all. so we fought by ourselves. sidekicking our way toward the shining light of the Hero Headquarters satellite in the stars. so many of us never made it. we were just kids. what did we know of justice? what happens to a teenager whose identity is grown around a battle for something greater? dear Dick Grayson, what would you have been if you never met Bruce Wayne? would it have been better or worse? i still can't decide. thirty years of the struggle and i'm still that kid, scanning the skyline for someone to swoop down and teach me to fly. and yet another part of me knows i'm too old for that kid stuff now. i fly on my own just fine.

Play a song for the child in you.

to the outlaws

We become outlaws one at a time. It is a lonely and terrifying experience. What we do offends explicit or implicit rules of belonging that regulate the ordinary world. Who we are contradicts the roles. . . . Under the laws of the Roman Empire, an outlaw lost rights as a citizen and became a "homo sacer" (sacred man). Theirs was a consecrated life, intended for special purpose, set apart and forbidden.

— CAFFYN JESSE, "Ethics for Outlaws"

once there was a village called Love. its denizens named it after an ancient goddess whose body was torn apart by the god of the sun, who feared that her power and beauty would be his undoing. and that village once contained a library full of poetry and a temple full of songs, but those were long since burned down by the citizens of Love, who had come to bitter disagreement about the best way to honor Love's memory. so they destroyed the library of Love and the temple of Love, they wrote terrible laws and made terrible wars, they policed and punished one another, all in Love's name.

when we left the village, we left one at a time. the only way to leave Love was alone. when you broke Love's laws, you lost all you had: your belongings, your belonging, your family, your name. the people of Love threw stones at us; they wrote their secrets and their shame on the stones and drew our blood with them so they could be free of the weight they kept in their souls. it did not work. our blood fell like rain, but their souls remained heavy. they made monsters of our bodies, but they did not become beautiful. there was always a new monster to drive out of Love.

so we fled to the woods, we monsters, lawbreakers, dwellers in darkness, fearsome freaks, and sacred homos. beyond the circle of village fires, we discovered the magic of the trees. we relearned the taste of the sacred herbs. we shed our scars and discovered new skins. in the outlaw space, we made new homes, places full of poetry and song. and yes, we hurt one another too, because the woods made us no

less dangerous. we were still monsters there. but we were
no longer alone.

the village was discontent. the denizens of Love could not
stop their children from breaking its laws. the children left
to find what was missing, and so in their anger and fear, the
denizens of Love blamed us. they took to the woods with
torches and dogs, with weapons and cages. they cut down
the trees and set fire to our homes, they caught us and
killed us in Love's name. but the woods were deep and the
shadows were long, and children kept breaking the laws
and leaving the village, and so the story of the outlaws
lives on.

you come to us now with scars on your skin. your blood is
freshly spilled and your name so recently taken. dear
outlaw, the time has come to choose your journey. dear
monster, it's time to choose your new shape. dear fearsome
freak, dear sacred homo, dear magic maker and
lawbreaker, what will you choose? to return to the village
or dwell in the woods? there is no safety in the circle of

village fires, but i can promise you no safety here either, in the shadows of the trees. i can promise you wonder. i can promise you freedom. i can promise you kinship, and heartbreak, and the ancient rituals of grief and repair. the village is poisoning itself from the inside out. the woods are being cut down around us. and yet i still believe in the ancient one, in the poems and the songs, in the beauty of monsters and the power of story, in the ghosts between us, in the outlaw realm, in the magic that still lives in me and my kindred—and in you, my love, in you.

Decide what's more important to you: safety or freedom. Discuss with a friend.

to the ones this world was never made for

i've never worried about dying. it's the world we live in that i
fear, and all the things i might have to see before it ends. the
things that people do to one another, and the things i might
do to others. i read in a book that when lightning strikes a
person, it leaves Lichtenberg figures on their skin—scars in
the shape of electric currents. the lightning still lives inside
them, and sometimes it changes their personality. sometimes
it causes phantom pains and memory loss, the uncontrollable
spasming of limbs. sometimes it grants mysterious gifts, like a
genius talent for playing piano or the ability to foretell the
weather. i think this is what violence does to the soul. the
other day i watched a stand-up comedy special in which the
comedian told joke after joke about how trans people are
apparently harming our allies and our own by fighting for our
human rights. it wasn't very funny, but it did make me cry. as
i listened to the comedian, i could feel the violence still
burning in the place where it entered my soul, and i could

hear where the violence had entered his. he says he doesn't hate people like me, and i believe him, but hate has almost never been the reason that humans hurt humans. fear is. i spend a lot of time these days thinking about the kind of person i want to be and all the courage it will take to get there. today i looked inside the ocean of my sadness and found a volcano of anger there. the lava said, *i am the courageous part of love*. where in the body does courage call home? the same place where lightning lives. *cuers* is Old French, meaning "heart." *rage* is also Old French, meaning "fury." what does that tell us about what it means to be brave? choosing love is a practice. every day it takes all my strength. still, i believe in this body, this soul, this fallible flesh that still burns with wanting. somewhere, after the lightning strikes, there will be a world for us.

Draw a compass. At each point, write down one value. These should be the values that are most dear to you. Think: If you were to die tomorrow, what would you want people to remember about you?

to me, from a revolutionary trans femme of color living in the distant future

and all they know of hate
is that it couldn't beat the love out of me . . .

—ANDREA GIBSON, "Ashes"

tonight, i am looking up at the stars and thinking of you. through the smoke from the fires that continue to ravage all life on this planet, i can still see the light of the heavens. i like to imagine you there, looking back. i wonder what you must think, seeing all that's happened since you were alive. since you fought for your freedom, and for ours, with a band of fierce and fabulous sisters. weird siblings. brothers grim and gay. i wish i could have been there. i wish i could have known you through more than the scraps of poetry and story your generation left behind. so many cycles have passed, so many empires that rose and fell, taking our history and our so-called progress with it. i want you to know how sacred you are. how much it means to us that you existed at all, that you left evidence behind, that you lived and breathed and hurt and hoped. i want you to know that we didn't win, not exactly, but we took the stories you and your brethren left behind and wove them into a new way of being. we never stopped hurting, but we learned how to heal. we never stopped harming one another, but we learned how to grow through our wounding in honesty and forgiveness. we developed the secret technology you dreamed about—the sacred ways of loving that can transform pain into pleasure, violence into grace. i want so much to make you proud. there are still those who hate us, who hunt us, who cannot bear their own incompleteness and therefore try to destroy us. there are still those who only know how to burn and destroy. and in the end, it may be that the burning appetite of those hungry ghosts will swallow us all. but you taught us that even ashes are sacred. flowers still grow from the scars in the earth marred by poisonous flames. love still endures. love survives. love revives. love redeems. love forgives. space and time themselves might end and the essence of what we are would still remain in a place beyond reckoning. wait for us there. we are coming.

Never forget who you are.

Acknowledgments

I am deeply grateful to the many people without whom I could not have written *Falling Back in Love with Being Human*. First and foremost, I would like to thank my incredible agents and champions, Marilyn Biderman and Léonicka Valcius, whose enthusiasm, patience, compassion, and love of literature were paramount in helping me to believe I even had another book to write — let alone bringing it to publication. I would also like to thank my editors, David Ross of Penguin Random House Canada and Katy Nishimoto of The Dial Press, for believing in my vision, and whose sharp eyes for detail and creative ingenuity have made this book much clearer and brighter than its original form. Special thanks to Katy and David as well for helping develop a new (and better) title for the work! Thank you to my teams at Penguin Canada and The Dial Press for all of your work: Whitney Frick, Debbie Aroff, Jordan Forney, Rachel Parker, Avideh

Bashirrad, Andy Ward, Donna Cheng, Leah Sims, Cara DuBois, Simon Sullivan, Amelia Zalcman, Deb Foley, Rebecca Berlant, Samuel Wetzler, Nicole Winstanley, Bonnie Maitland, Daniel French, and Chalista Andadari.

There are many writers, thinkers, and artists to whom I am indebted. I have so much gratitude for K. A. Applegate, creator of the Animorphs series, who shaped my childhood and continues to influence my outlook on the world today. I am grateful as well to the Black and POC queer feminist lineage of abolitionist thinkers and writers, including Mariame Kaba, Shira Hassan, adrienne maree brown, Autumn Brown, Leah Lakshmi Piepzna-Samarasinha, Mia Mingus, and many more, who continue to dream of and fight for freedom. I am similarly grateful to the lineage of trans feminine and transsexual woman writers, thinkers, and fighters, including Sandy Stone, Viviane Namaste, Morgan M Page, Kama La Mackerel, Nina Arsenault, Mirha-Soleil Ross, Aiyyana Maracle, and many others. Thanks also to Caffyn Jesse, wise teacher and queer elder, and to the rest of our Conflict Coven Transformative Justice Collective.

In a strange way, I am also indebted to the many whose words and thoughts are often perceived as in opposition to people like me: J. K. Rowling, Jordan Peterson, Dave Chappelle, Meghan Murphy, Janice Raymond, and more. I do not agree with you. But I still want to know how and why we have come to this place with one another. I still believe that we can find a way to understand one another. You, too, are my teachers in love.

Thank you, finally, to Emily, Kelly, Kama, Andrew, and Kota—my dear queer chosen family, who have always loved me. Thank you to Amber Dawn and Chanelle, beloved mentor femmes. And thank you to Jacob, spouse, goblin royalty, and greatest love, whom I so rarely write poems about. You keep me alive and in love.

About the Author

KAI CHENG THOM is an award-winning writer, performance artist, and community healer in Toronto. She was a finalist for the Lambda Literary Award and won the Writers' Trust of Canada's Dayne Ogilvie Prize for LGBTQ2S+ Emerging Writers for her surrealist novel, *Fierce Femmes and Notorious Liars: A Dangerous Trans Girl's Confabulous Memoir*. She is also the author of several other books, including a poetry collection, an essay collection, and two children's picture books. Kai Cheng writes the advice column "Ask Kai: Advice for the Apocalypse" for *Xtra*.

kaichengthom.com
Twitter: @razorfemme
Instagram: @kaichengthom

*The Dial Press, an imprint of Random House,
publishes books driven by the heart.*

Follow us on Instagram:
@THEDIALPRESS

Discover other Dial Press books and sign up for our e-newsletter:

thedialpress.com